United States Presidents

Theodore Roosevelt

Anne Welsbacher
ABDO Publishing Company

visit us at
www.abdopub.com

Published by Abdo Publishing Company 4940 Viking Drive, Edina, Minnesota 55435.

Printed in the United States.

Cover and Interior Photo credits: Peter Arnold, Inc., SuperStock, Archive, Corbis-Bettmann

Edited by Lori Kinstad Pupeza
Contributing editor Brooke Henderson

Library of Congress Cataloging-in-Publication Data

Welsbacher, Anne, 1955-
Theodore Roosevelt / Anne Welsbacher.
p. cm. -- (United States presidents)
Includes index.
ISBN 1-56239-742-7
1. Roosevelt, Theodore, 1858-1919--Juvenile literature. 2. Presidents--United States--Biography--Juvenile literature. [1. Roosevelt, Theodore, 1858-1919. 2. Presidents.] I. Title. II. Series: United States presidents (Edina, Minn.)
E757.W48 1998
973.91'1'092--dc21
[B] 98-4808
CIP
AC

Contents

Theodore Roosevelt

Theodore Roosevelt was the 26th president of the United States. He was the youngest president. He was full of energy and life.

Theodore Roosevelt set up the national park system. He made new laws to protect workers. He worked for safer food and drug rules.

Theodore Roosevelt loved to hunt, see the world, and fight in battles. He also helped bring peace between two countries. He won a Nobel Peace Prize.

Theodore Roosevelt was born in New York. Growing up he studied animals and insects. He traveled to many countries and read many books.

Theodore went to Harvard **University**. He married Alice Hathaway Lee. But she died while giving birth. He moved to a ranch in North Dakota for two years and worked hard to recover from his sadness.

Theodore Roosevelt campaigning for McKinley during his Presidential campaign.

He married Edith Carow and had many children. He was head of New York's police and head of the U.S. government workers. He fought dishonest people and passed many laws to make it harder to cheat people.

He fought a big battle in Cuba during a war with Spain. Later he was elected Governor of New York. Soon he was chosen to be vice president of the United States!

When President McKinley was killed, Theodore Roosevelt became President. He worked for a "square deal" for all Americans. He made new laws to protect mine workers. He fought against dishonest owners of railroad companies.

Theodore Roosevelt wanted all future Americans to enjoy nature and animals. He made laws to keep millions of acres of land as parks. These make up the national park system.

Theodore Roosevelt traveled to Africa where he hunted wild animals. He traveled to Brazil, where he became sick. Theodore Roosevelt died at age 60.

Opposite page: Theodore Roosevelt campaigning for the Presidency in 1904.

Theodore Roosevelt (1858-1919)
Twenty-sixth President

BORN:	October 27, 1858
PLACE OF BIRTH:	New York, New York
ANCESTRY:	English, Dutch, Scotch, Huguenot
FATHER:	Theodore Roosevelt (1831-1878)
MOTHER:	Martha Bulloch Roosevelt (1834-1884)
WIVES:	First wife: Alice Hathaway Lee (1861-1884)
	Second wife: Edith Kermit Carow (1861-1948)
CHILDREN:	First wife, one girl
	Second wife, five: 4 boys, 1 girl
EDUCATION:	Private tutoring; 1876-1880 Harvard (B.A.); studied law at Columbia
RELIGION:	Dutch Reformed
OCCUPATION:	Writer, historian, rancher
MILITARY SERVICE:	Lieutenant Colonel, Colonel, 1st U.S. Volunteers Cavalry Regiment (Rough Riders) 1898
POLITICAL PARTY:	Republican

OFFICES HELD:	New York State Assemblyman; U.S. Civil Service Commissioner; President of New York Board of Police Commissioners; Assistant Secretary of the Navy; Governor of New York State; Vice President
AGE AT INAUGURATION:	42
TERMS SERVED:	Two (1901-1905) (1905-1909)
VICE PRESIDENT:	First term: None. Second term: Charles W. Fairbanks (1905-1909)
DIED:	January 6, 1919, Oyster Bay, New York, age 60
CAUSE OF DEATH:	Coronary embolism

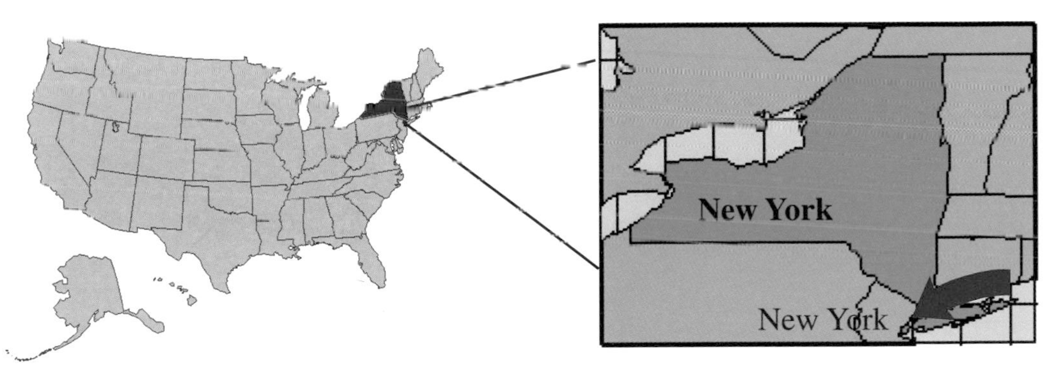

Birthplace of Theodore Roosevelt

Early Years

Theodore Roosevelt was born on October 27, 1858, in New York, New York. His nickname was "Teddie." His father, Theodore Sr., was a **millionaire**. His mother, Martha Bulloch, was from Georgia.

As a child, Teddie was very sick with asthma. Sometimes he couldn't breathe, and his family was afraid he would die. Because he was so weak, he studied at home. He read many books.

He loved to collect insects, mice, snakes, and other animals. He kept their bodies in his room and wrote down everything about them. He called his collection "The Roosevelt Museum of Natural History!"

Despite the work of many doctors, he was still very sick. When he was 10, his father told him to try to build a strong body all by himself. Teddie agreed. He learned to box, lifted weights, hiked, and swam.

Slowly he got stronger. His hard work paid off! At 16, Theodore studied to go to Harvard **University**.

Portrait of Theodore Roosevelt at age 10.

Harvard

Theodore was 18 when he went to Harvard. He still studied animals and now had hundreds in his collection. He also danced, rowed boats, swam, ran races, high jumped, and fought in a boxing match.

Theodore always did everything with energy! He asked lots of questions in class. He loved to talk. He told jokes at parties and made people laugh.

In 1878, Theodore's father died of cancer. Theodore was very sad. He decided to work to be someone important in memory of his father.

In his second year of college, Theodore met Alice Hathaway Lee. He wanted to marry her, but she was not sure. Not long after, he wrote a book about the War of 1812. Theodore wrote many more books all his life.

In 1880, Theodore finished Harvard. Alice finally agreed to be his wife. They were married on his 22nd birthday, October 27, 1880.

That year Theodore went to Columbia Law School. He met many working people and learned about unfair things that happened to them. Soon he was working in **politics** to help change those things.

An 1880 portrait of Theodore Roosevelt as a student at Harvard.

Jack-in-the-Box

In November 1881, Theodore was elected to the New York assembly, a group in **politics**. He asked many questions and had many ideas. One newspaper writer said that the way he always jumped up with questions, he was just like a Jack-in-the-Box!

In February 1884, Alice gave birth to a baby girl. But two days later she died from childbirth. The same day, Theodore's mother died of typhoid fever.

Theodore was so sad he left New York. His sister took care of his baby daughter. He went to a ranch in North Dakota.

Theodore worked as a cowboy for two years. He wrote books and bought land there. He hunted bison and helped the sheriff chase outlaws!

In 1885 he came home to New York. Soon he fell in love with his childhood best friend, Edith Carow. He ran for mayor of New York, but he lost. In December 1886, Theodore and Edith were married.

Edith and Theodore had five children, and Alice was the daughter of Theodore and Alice. Theodore loved to play with his six children. Together they ran through the house, shouted, and laughed.

President Roosevelt is photographed with his family at their home in 1907.

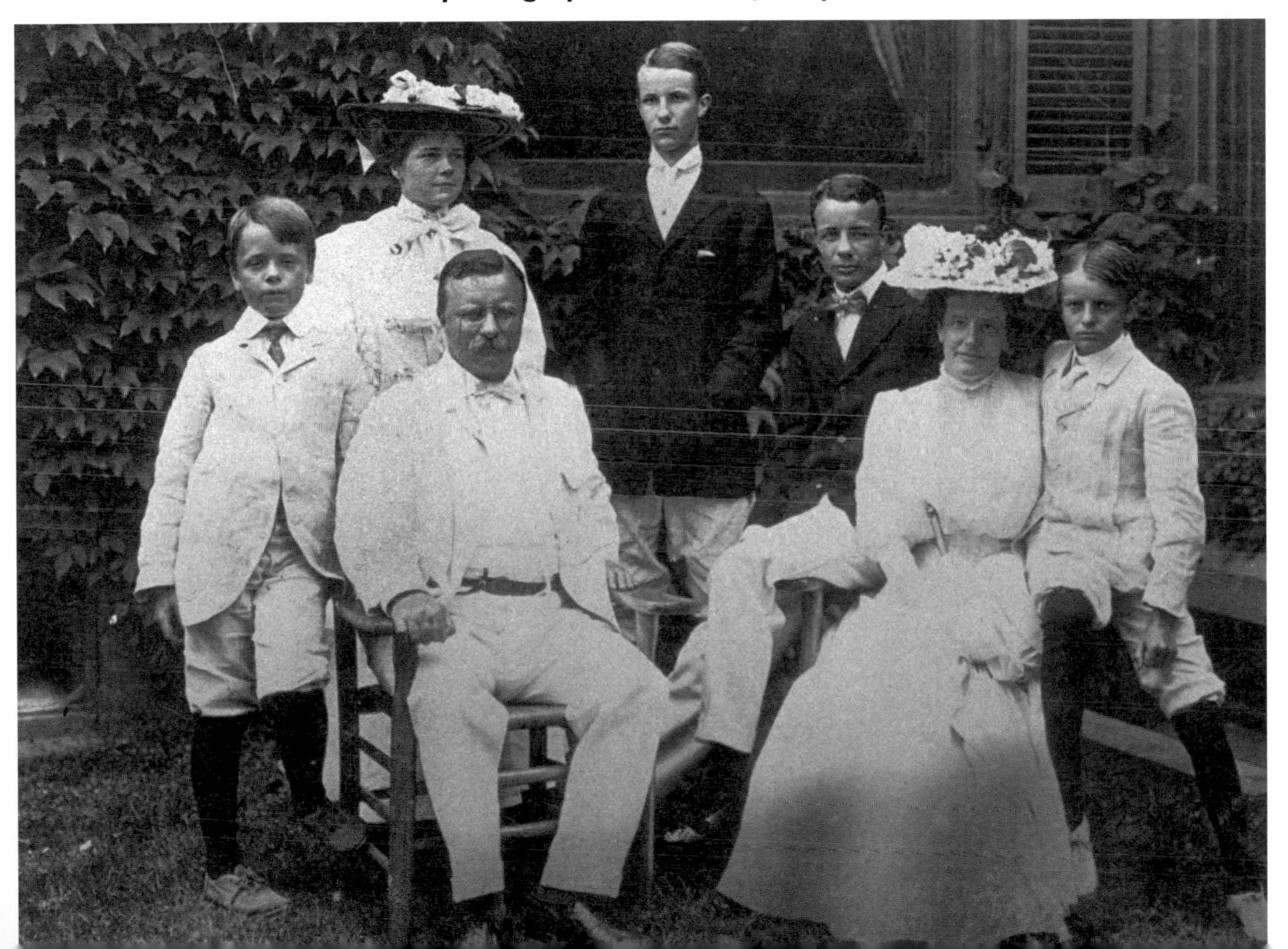

The Making of the 26th United States President

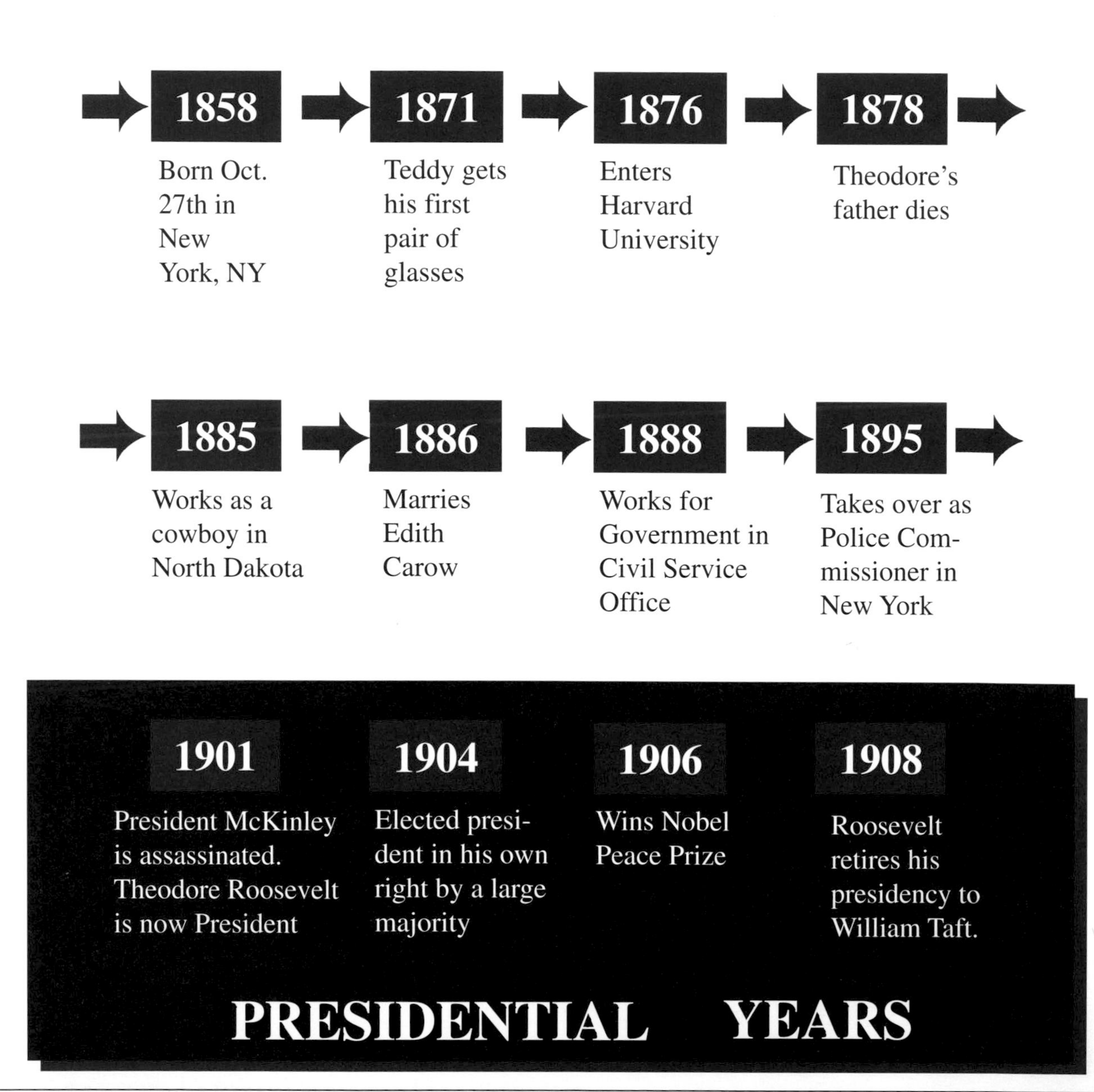

Theodore Roosevelt

"It is well indeed for our land that we of this generation have learned to think nationally."

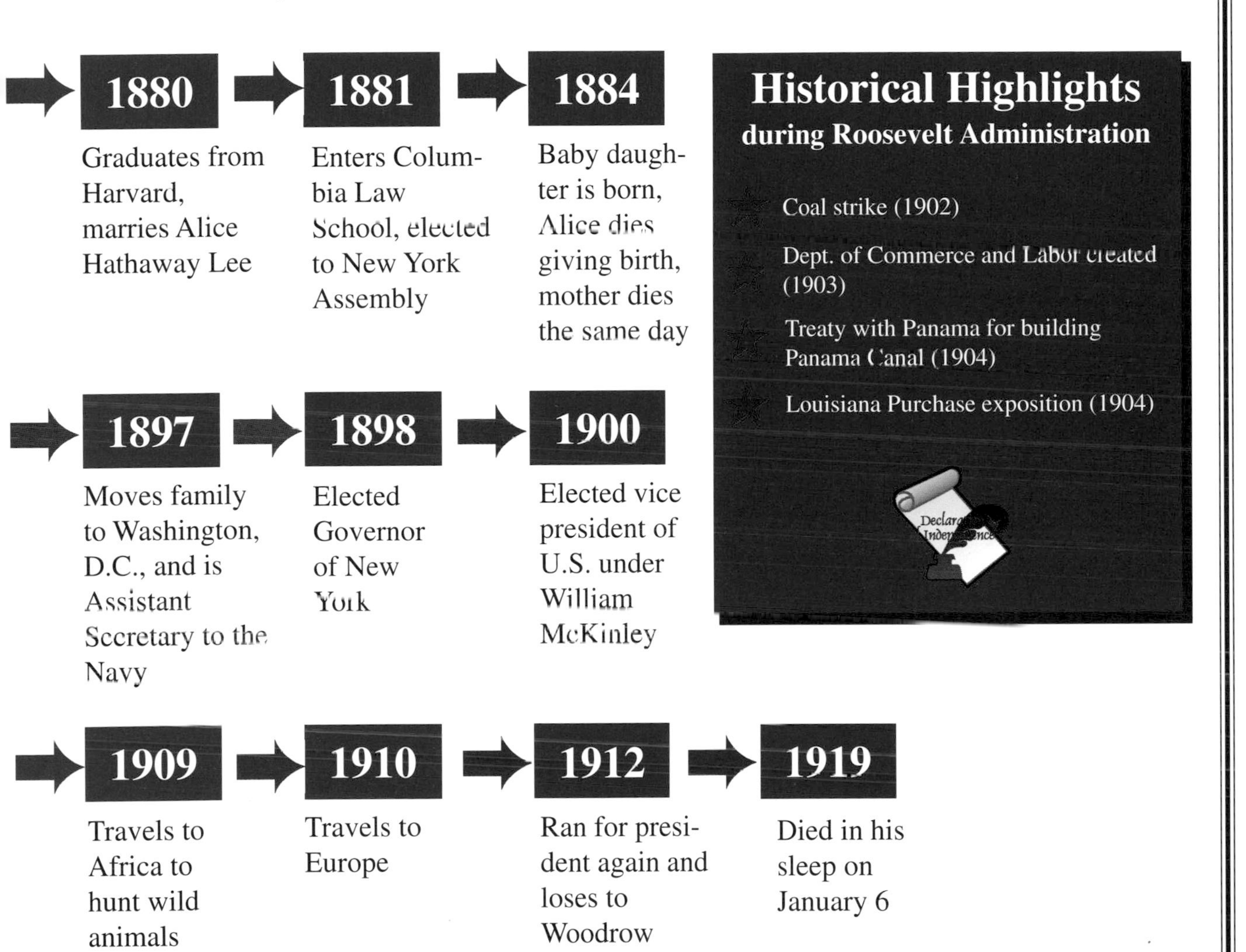

Theodore the Reformer

In 1888, the President of the United States asked Theodore to lead the **civil service** office. Civil service jobs are jobs in the government.

There were many dishonest people in the government. Theodore worked to change this. He fired dishonest people. He made the government a better place to work.

Soon he was asked to be the head of the New York Police. Once again, he worked to end dishonesty. He dressed up in disguise and watched police officers to make sure they were doing their jobs right. He fired more people—even the chief of police!

Theodore wanted William McKinley to be the next president of the U.S. In the summer of 1896, he **campaigned** for McKinley.

McKinley won the election. But Theodore was winning, too. His hard work and his campaign made people all over America start to notice Theodore Roosevelt!

Theodore Roosevelt working in a civil service job.

A Rough Rider

President McKinley made Theodore the assistant secretary to the Navy. In 1897, Theodore and his family moved to Washington, D.C. Theodore loved battles and ships, and he was excited about his new job.

At that time, Spain and Cuba were at war. Theodore wanted to help Cuba fight against Spain. While the secretary of the Navy was out of town, Theodore ordered ships to Spanish ports. This made many people angry.

In February 1898, Spain blew up a U.S. ship, and the U.S. decided to go to war against Spain. Theodore quit his job and went to Cuba to fight in the war.

Theodore trained men to help him fight against Cuba. They were all a little wild, like him. People called his men "Roosevelt's Rough Riders." On July 1, 1898, the Rough Riders charged up Kettle Hill in Cuba and won a battle. Then they charged up San Juan Hill and won another battle!

Cuba won the war two weeks later. When Theodore Roosevelt came home, Americans welcomed him as a hero.

In the fall of 1898, Theodore was elected Governor of New York. He helped shorten long working hours for children. He made laws that forced big companies to pay their share of taxes.

In 1900, William McKinley ran for president of the United States, with Theodore as vice president. In November, McKinley was elected president, and Theodore Roosevelt was the new vice president.

But in September 1901, only six months later, President McKinley was shot and killed. Theodore Roosevelt was the new president of the United States. He was only 42, the youngest man ever to be president.

The inauguration of President Theodore Roosevelt, 1905.

President Roosevelt

Many things were happening in the United States while Roosevelt was president. Big companies charged unfair prices and didn't pay their workers enough money. Theodore forced these big companies to change.

Workers in mines had unsafe jobs. Sometimes they were hurt in the mines, and they had to work more than 12 hours every day! They tried to form groups that would demand fair rules from the mine owners.

Theodore helped the groups, called unions, talk to the owners. He also created a new government group to help workers get a fair deal. Theodore called this a "square deal."

Theodore also passed laws to get a **canal** built around the country of Panama. A canal is a small river made by people. The Panama Canal made it easier and faster for ships to carry things from one country to another.

In 1903, Theodore set aside Pelican Island in Florida to be a park. Later he created Yosemite National Park and other parks in

Theodore Roosevelt delivering another fiery address to a crowd of 50,000 on July 21, 1915.

the Southwest. During his presidency, Theodore Roosevelt set aside 125 million acres of land for parks around the country.

In 1904, Theodore Roosevelt was elected president. He continued to work for **reform**. In 1906 he passed a new law called the Pure Food and Drug Act. It forced meat packers to make sure the meat they sold to people was safe to eat.

In 1905, Russia and Japan were about to go to war. Theodore Roosevelt brought them together to talk. The two countries decided not to go to war because of Theodore Roosevelt. In 1906, he won the Nobel Peace Prize for keeping this war from happening.

In 1908, Theodore Roosevelt **campaigned** for William Taft for President. Taft won the election, and 50-year-old Theodore left the White House for new adventures.

Opposite page: President Theodore Roosevelt pictured in the White House in 1908.

Bull Moose Adventurer

In March 1909, Theodore went to Africa to hunt wild animals. His son and many scientists and writers went with him. He killed 500 animals and birds. He gave most of them to the Smithsonian museum in Washington, D.C.

In 1910 he traveled to Europe. He met kings and famous people in Germany, Sweden, and England. Finally, in June 1910, he returned home to New York.

In 1912 he decided to run for president again! But this time he ran in a new political party, called the Progressive Party. People called it the Bull Moose party because Theodore was wild like a bull moose!

Theodore lost the election to Democrat Woodrow Wilson. In 1913, he wrote another book, the story of his life. Then he traveled to the Grand Canyon with his sons.

In January 1914, Theodore had his last big adventure. He traveled to Brazil. He hiked through jungles and took boats down rivers. But he fell from his boat and cut himself. The cut got infected and he got sick.

By 1918, Theodore was in bad health. He went to the hospital with an ear infection and a disease called rheumatism. On January 6, 1919, Theodore Roosevelt died. He was 60 years old.

Theodore Roosevelt is shown beside this elephant he brought down in Africa in 1909.

Fun Facts

•Theodore Roosevelt's children were called "The White House Gang." They roller-skated all through the White House, walked around on stilts, raced up and down the stairs, and slid down the banisters!

•Once when Theodore was hunting in Mississippi, he saw a bear cub. He did not shoot it because it was just a baby. Newspapers took pictures of him with the bear, and soon stores invented new toys—soft, stuffed bears. They called them "teddy bears."

•In October 1901, President Roosevelt invited the famous leader Booker T. Washington to dinner at the White House. It was the first time an African American ate dinner at the White House as a guest.

•Women in the United States did not win the right to vote until 1922. But 44 years earlier, in 1878, Theodore Roosevelt wrote a paper arguing that women should vote. In 1912, when he ran for President under the Bull Moose party, Theodore again argued for women's right to vote.

•Theodore Roosevelt loved to read. Before he learned to read, when he was only 2 or 3, he looked at pictures. But soon he knew all the pictures and wanted to learn more about them. So he went all through the house asking grownups to read to him and teach him words. As a grownup, he sometimes read a new book every day!

•Theodore Roosevelt once said the best way to bring changes was to "speak softly and carry a big stick." He learned these words from an African saying.

•As a boy, Teddie kept a large collection of dead animals—along with skins, wings, and other parts—in his bedroom. But the creatures turned up in other places too. He once asked the family cook to boil a dead woodchuck for a day. She would not do it! Another time he lifted his hat to say hello to a friend. A frog popped out!

Roosevelt with the Rough Riders.

Glossary

Campaign—to make speeches, write letters, or travel around the country asking people to vote for you or somebody else.

Canal—a small river made by people.

Civil service—work for the state or United States government.

Inauguration—a ceremony that begins the president's term. The inauguration takes place a few months after a president is elected. The president makes a speech promising to do the best he can, and after the speech there is a big party.

Millionaire—a person who has millions of dollars.

Politics—the process of making laws and running a government.

Reform—to change something that seems wrong into something that seems better.

University—a school you can go to after high school.

Veteran—a person who fought in a war; after the war in Cuba, the Rough Riders were veterans.

Internet Sites

United States Presidents Information Page
http://we.got.net/docent/soquel/prez.htm
Links to information about United States Presidents. This site is very informative, with biographies on every president as well as speeches and debates, and other links.

The Presidents of the United States of America
http://www.whitehouse.gov/WH/glimpse/presidents/html/presidents.html
This site is from the White House. With an introduction from President Bill Clinton and biographies that include each president's inaugural address, this site is excellent. Get White House History information, Art in the White House, First Ladies, First Families, and much more.

POTUS—Presidents of the United States
http://www.ipl.org/ref/POTUS/
In this web site you will find background information, election results, cabinet members, presidency highlights, and some odd facts on each of the presidents. Links to biographies, historical documents, audio and video files, and other presidential sites are also included to enrich this site.

These sites are subject to change. Go to your favorite search engine and type in United States Presidents for more sites.

Index